BRILLIANT PEOPLE, BIG IDEAS

MISTAKES

Written by Rebecca Phillips-Bartlett

BookLife PUBLISHING

©2023
BookLife Publishing Ltd.
King's Lynn, Norfolk
PE30 4LS, UK

All facts, statistics, web addresses and URLs in this book were verified as valid and accurate at time of writing. No responsibility for any changes to external websites or references can be accepted by either the author or publisher.

All rights reserved.
Printed in China.

A catalogue record for this book is available from the British Library.

HB ISBN: 978-1-80505-010-0
PB ISBN: 978-1-80505-380-4

Written by:
Rebecca Phillips-Bartlett

Edited by:
Kirsty Holmes

Designed by:
Isabella Croker

FSC MIX Paper from responsible sources FSC® C113515

Image Credits

All images are courtesy of Shutterstock.com, unless otherwise specified. With thanks to Getty Images, Thinkstock Photo and iStockphoto.

Recurring images – Andrew Rybalko, cosmaa, davooda, P-fotography, Mark Rademaker. Cover – davooda, Andrew Rybalko, dimair, cosmaa, P-fotography. 2–3 – Nastya Trel, Cofefe. 4–5 – Sharomka. 6–7 – Materialscientist, Top Vector Studio, Tatahnka, Yeti studio. 8–9 – Net Vector, LuYago, Lilanakani, Siberian Art, Materialscientist. 10–11 – Kateryna Kon, Ducksoup. 12–13 – ApoGapo, Prostorina, Cofefe, ZOVICOTA. 14–15 – robuart, Andrei Kuzmik, Svetlana_Smirnova. 16–17 – Biscotto Design, Nastya Trel, AlenKadr. 18–19 – Dzm1try, Lyudmyla Kharlamova. 20–21 – Stocksnapper, Ekaterina_Minaeva, futuristman, Vladimir Konstantinov. 22–23 – Narint Asawaphisith, stockpexel.

Contents

Page 4	Big Ideas
Page 6	George Crum and Kate Speck Wicks
Page 8	Wilhelm Conrad Röntgen
Page 10	Alexander Fleming
Page 12	Percy Spencer
Page 14	Frank Epperson
Page 16	Ruth Graves Wakefield
Page 18	Dr Spencer Silver and Arthur Fry
Page 20	The Hall of Fame
Page 22	All You Need Is an Idea!
Page 24	Glossary and Index

Words that look like this can be found in the glossary on page 24.

Big Ideas

Think of all the amazing <u>inventions</u> you use in a day. Someone very clever must have invented all these gadgets, right?

George Crum and Kate Speck Wicks

"One of us <u>accidentally</u> invented crisps."

1822–1924

"But no one can remember who it was…"

1824–1914

Crisps !?

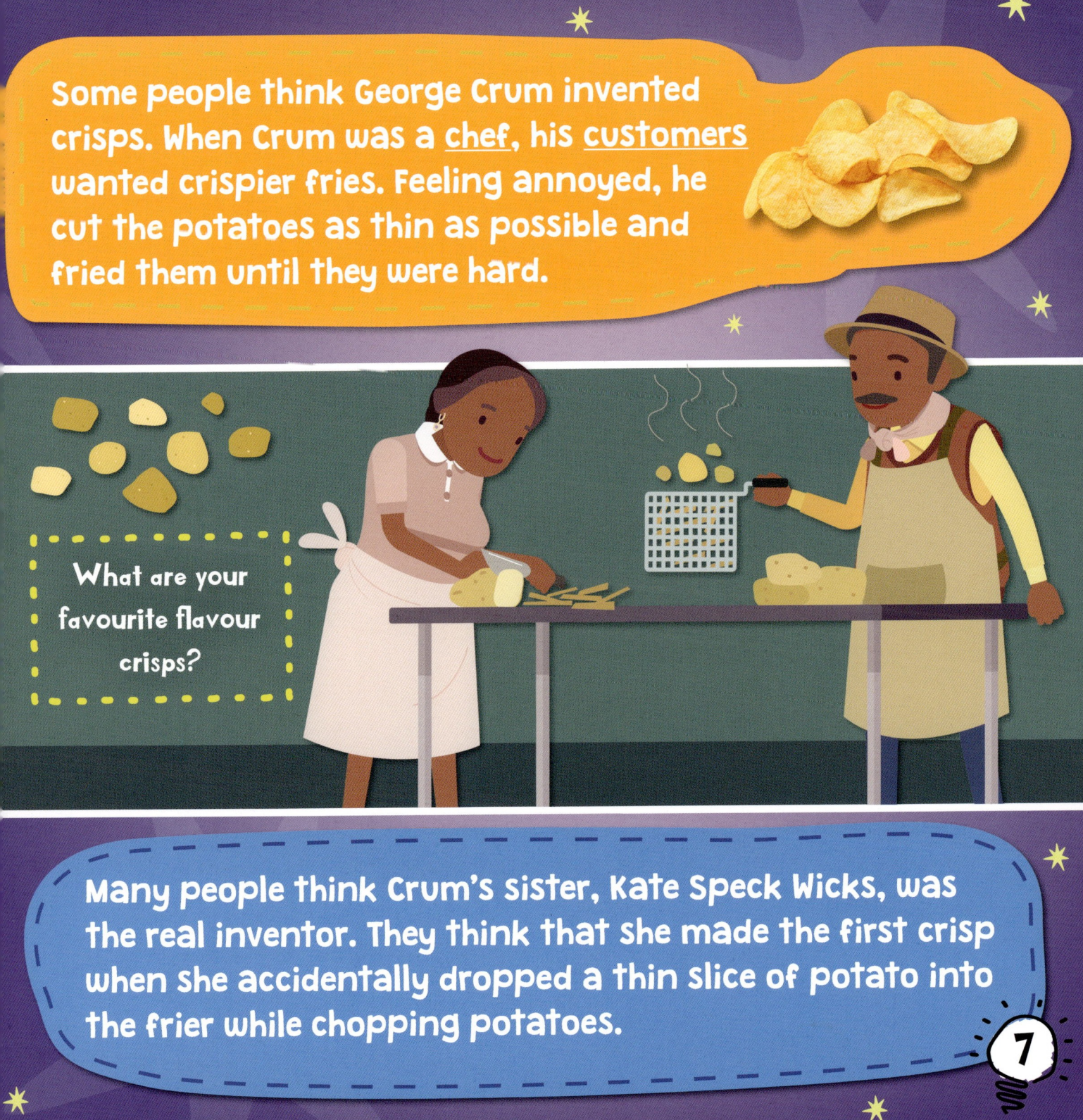

Some people think George Crum invented crisps. When Crum was a <u>chef</u>, his <u>customers</u> wanted crispier fries. Feeling annoyed, he cut the potatoes as thin as possible and fried them until they were hard.

What are your favourite flavour crisps?

Many people think Crum's sister, Kate Speck Wicks, was the real inventor. They think that she made the first crisp when she accidentally dropped a thin slice of potato into the frier while chopping potatoes.

Wilhelm Conrad Röntgen

1845–1923

I was working in my <u>laboratory</u> when I noticed something unexpected!

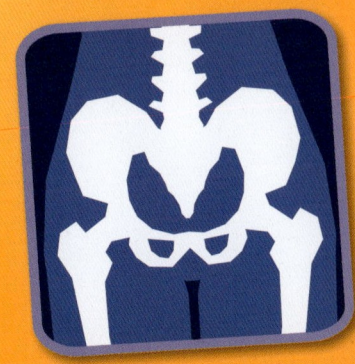

X-Rays

Wilhelm Conrad Röntgen was a scientist studying special types of light. He noticed that when he took a photo of his wife's hand using the light, he could see her bones!

Have you ever had an X-ray?

Röntgen called this type of light an X-ray. Röntgen's accident changed the world of medicine. Today, doctors use X-rays to help people with broken bones.

Alexander Fleming

I forgot to do the washing up before I left my laboratory, but I found something amazing when I returned!

1881–1955

Penicillin

Alexander Fleming was doing an <u>experiment</u> with dishes of <u>bacteria</u>. He went away and left the dishes in the window. When he came back, the dishes were mouldy!

Fleming noticed that the bacteria near the mould were dying. This mould made a new medicine called penicillin. What a good thing he did not bother to wash up!

Have you ever spotted mould growing on something?

Percy Spencer

I was working as an engineer when I made a tasty mistake!

1894–1970

Microwave Ovens

Percy Spencer was an engineer. One day he noticed that, when he stood next to a special machine called a radar set, the chocolate bar in his pocket melted!

Spencer realised that part of the radar, called a magnetron, could be used to cook food. Soon he was snacking on the world's first-ever microwave popcorn!

Spencer's discovery led to the microwave. What other food can you cook in a microwave?

Frank Epperson

1894–1983

I was only 11 years old when I invented ice pops!

Ice Pops

After playing outside during the day, 11-year-old Frank Epperson forgot to take his drink inside. He left his drink and stirring stick outside overnight.

During the night, it got so cold that the drink froze. The next morning, curious Epperson ate his frozen drink. This was the first ice pop!

Epperson started selling his ice pops to his friends. What flavour ice pop would you buy?

Ruth Graves Wakefield

I am a chef. I love baking cookies!

1903–1977

Chocolate Chip Cookies

Some people believe that Ruth Graves Wakefield invented chocolate chip cookies by mistake! Wakefield wanted to bake whole chocolate cookies, but she had run out of the chocolate she normally used.

Have you ever made chocolate chip cookies?

Wakefield tried using small pieces of another kind of chocolate, expecting the chocolate to <u>melt</u>. The chocolate did not melt. Instead, it stayed in the cookies as chocolate chips. Wakefield had made chocolate chip cookies!

Dr Spencer Silver and Arthur Fry

1941–2021

1931–now

We are both scientists. We worked together to invent sticky notes!

Sticky Notes

Dr Spencer Silver was trying to make a new, strong glue. However, he accidentally made a glue that was not very sticky or strong at all.

Meanwhile, Arthur Fry had been getting annoyed that his bookmarks kept falling out. He remembered hearing about Silver's glue and thought it could keep his bookmarks in place. Together, Silver and Fry invented sticky notes.

The Hall of Fame

There are lots of other inventions which were invented by mistake. Here are some other inventions that no one planned!

Ice Cream Cones

There are many stories about who might have invented ice cream cones. One story says that an ice cream seller ran out of tubs, so started selling ice creams in wafers.

Hook and Loop

George de Mestral got covered in burs from a plant. He studied the plants to find out what made them stick so well and invented hook and loop fastenings based on these plants!

Burs

Playdough

Playdough was first invented for cleaning! After a while, people realised it made a great toy.

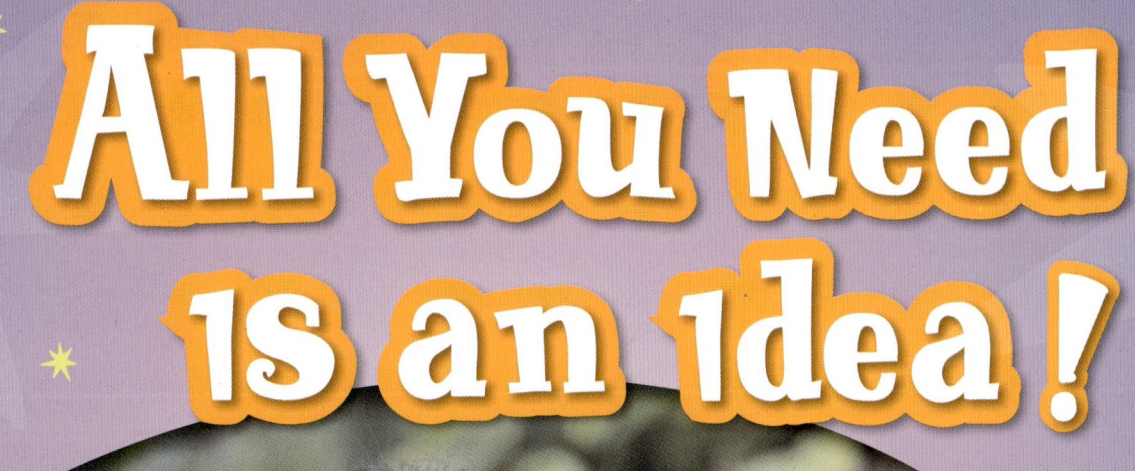

All You Need is an Idea!

From X-rays to ice pops, everything had to be invented, and that means that everything needed an inventor. All the inventors who came up with these things were brilliant and creative!

Even when things went wrong, these people used their creativity and strength to turn it into something amazing. All you need is one idea, and it could lead to lots of amazing discoveries!

What could you try to invent?

Glossary

accidentally	by mistake or not on purpose
bacteria	tiny living things, too small to see, that can cause diseases
chef	a person whose job it is to cook food
customers	people who visit somewhere, such as a restaurant or shop, and buy things
engineer	a person who designs and builds machines
experiment	trying or testing something new
fastenings	things that hold things closed
inventions	new things that are created
laboratory	a place where scientists work and do experiments
melt	when something is changed from a solid to a liquid
studied	learnt about

Index

chefs 7, 16
chocolate chip cookies 16–17
crisps 6–7
hook and loop 21
ice cream cones 20
ice pops 14–15, 22
microwaves 12–13
penicillin 10–11
playdough 21
popcorn 13
sticky notes 18–19
X-rays 8–9, 22